CONTENTS

WHY DO WE USE THE SUPREME COURT?

The United States federal government is broken into three separate but equal parts. The executive branch is made up of the president and a cabinet of advisors. The legislative branch is made up of Congress, which suggests and approves laws for American citizens to follow. The judicial branch is made up of courts and judges that decide whether a law has been broken or whether a law is inherently unfair.

The Supreme Court is the highest court in the nation. It makes important decisions about the rights of Americans. It makes its decisions based on what was written in the Constitution. The Bill of Rights is an addition to the Constitution, which includes important amendments such as the right to freedom of religion, speech, and the press. After the initial ten amendments, seventeen more were added. The most recent one was added in 1992.

SPOTLIGHT ON THE CIVIL RIGHTS MOVEMENT™

BROWN v. BOARD OF EDUCATION

KATHY FURGANG

Rosen YA™
New York

Published in 2018 by The Rosen Publishing Group, Inc.
29 East 21st Street, New York, NY 10010

First Edition

Library of Congress Cataloging-in-Publication Data

Names: Furgang, Kathy, author.
Title: Brown v. Board of Education / Kathy Furgang.
Description: New York : Rosen Publishing, 2018. | Series: Spotlight on the civil rights movement | Includes bibliographical references and index. | Audience: Grades 5–10.
Identifiers: LCCN 2017013316| ISBN 9781538380246 (library bound) | ISBN 9781538380215 (pbk.) | ISBN 9781538380222 (6 pack)
Subjects: LCSH: Brown, Oliver, 1918–1961—Trials, litigation, etc—Juvenile literature. | Topeka (Kan.). Board of Education—Trials, litigation, etc.—Juvenile literature. | Segregation in education—Law and legislation—United States—Juvenile literature.
Classification: LCC KF228.B76 F87 2017 | DDC 344.73/0798—dc23
LC record available at https://lccn.loc.gov/2017013316

Manufactured in China

On the cover: Without the landmark Supreme Court case of *Brown v. Board of Education*, classrooms like the one shown here would remain segregated today.

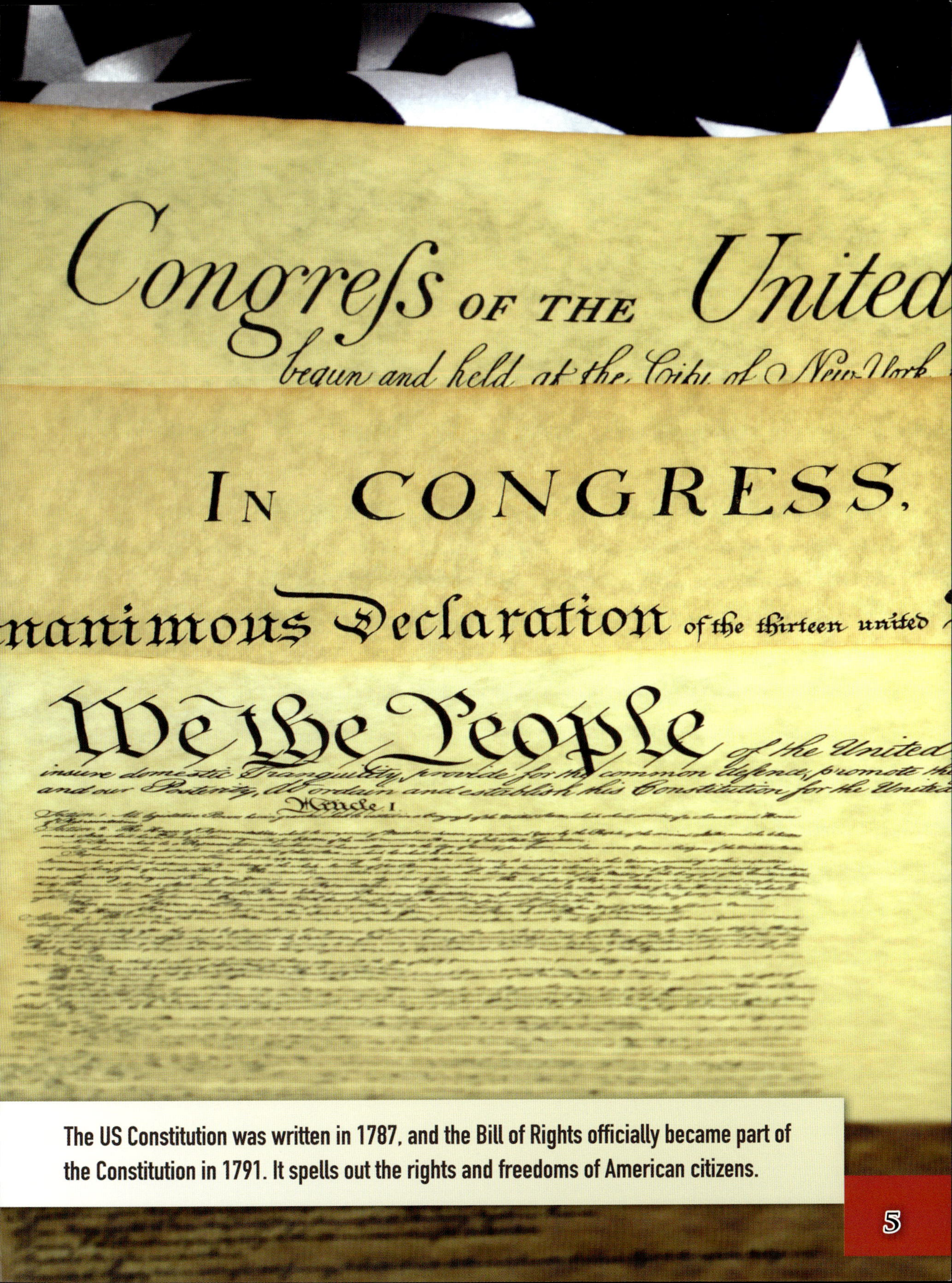

The US Constitution was written in 1787, and the Bill of Rights officially became part of the Constitution in 1791. It spells out the rights and freedoms of American citizens.

AN IMPORTANT CASE: DRED SCOTT

The Supreme Court analyzes the words of the nation's founders and makes decisions about what the Constitution and its amendments mean.

One of the earliest civil rights cases was called the Dred Scott case of 1857. During this time, states were still deciding whether slavery would be allowed in them. Some states allowed it, while others did not. A Missouri slave named Dred Scott went with his master, an officer in the army, to live in the free state of Illinois. Scott returned to Missouri with his master and then sued for his freedom after his master's death. He said he should be free because he had once lived in a free state. The court ruled that

Scott, as a slave, was not a citizen so he could not sue in a federal court. The case caused a greater rift between free states, mostly in the North, and the slave states, mostly in the South.

The Supreme Court case concerning Missouri slave Dred Scott was one of the first civil rights cases in the United States.

SEPARATE BUT EQUAL

The Civil War, in which the North fought the South, brought the problem of slavery to a head. The North won in 1865, and slavery was outlawed. Still, African Americans were treated poorly in many areas of the country, but especially in the South. In 1896, the Supreme Court decided an important case called *Plessy v. Ferguson*, which made it legal to segregate public areas, like schools, according to race. It stated that schools could accept white students only if black students had "separate but equal" facilities. This case made segregation legal.

The important Supreme Court cases of Dred Scott and *Plessy v. Ferguson* set the stage for the civil rights movement of the 1950s

Keith Plessy and Phoebe Ferguson are descendants of the people involved in the 1896 Supreme Court case, *Plessy v. Ferguson*.

and 1960s. *Brown v. Board of Education* was the next groundbreaking Supreme Court decision that would affect the lives of millions of Americans.

THE BROWN FAMILY

The 1954 landmark Supreme Court case *Brown v. Board of Education* began in the everyday life of the Brown family from Topeka, Kansas. The Browns, who were African American, lived in a neighborhood that was just five minutes from a local public school. However, they could not send their third-grade daughter, Linda, there because it was designated an all-white school. Instead, Linda had to walk a mile and cross a railroad switchyard to attend school at an all-black facility. The city of Topeka had eighteen schools for white children but only four for black children.

The Brown family decided to sue the state. They claimed that the city's black and white schools were not equal and that this fact made them unconstitutional. The Brown family took their legal battle to the courts of Kansas, which already had eleven cases challenging the fairness of schools for black children.

The case *Brown v. Board of Education* involved the civil rights of third grader Linda Brown (*far left*), shown here with her family on their front porch in 1953.

WHAT DID KANSAS DECIDE?

The state of Kansas sided against the families who were affected by the segregation. They stated that the schools met the "separate but equal" idea established in the case of *Plessy v. Ferguson*. Civil rights activists recognized that the case was being used as an excuse to continue the practice of segregation. Schools were not the only places affected. In many places, blacks had to sit in separate areas of restaurants and buses, as well as use different public pools and water fountains. The places that did this said that they were complying with the "separate but equal" law.

However, the Kansas court did recognize that segregation between white and black children in public schools had a negative effect upon black children. They acknowledged that this

These bathrooms were built on an outdoor construction site in Tennessee that was used in 1943. They show the effects of the "separate but equal" ruling of the *Plessy v. Ferguson* court case.

effect was greater when segregation was the law. So even though the case was lost, there was reason enough to bring it to the highest court in the nation—the Supreme Court.

OTHER CIVIL RIGHTS EDUCATION CASES

The Browns' case was not the only one being presented to the Supreme Court. The case *Brown v. Board of Education* was actually a combination of four cases from Kansas, South Carolina, and Virginia. A court case in Delaware had a different outcome. It stated that the plaintiff's rights had been violated due to the inferiority of black schools.

Other cases included one from South Carolina in which black students had no bus transportation. Some had to walk as far as eight miles (thirteen kilometers) to and from school. In the District of Columbia, schools built for black students were not kept "equal" to the white schools. They were overcrowded and there were no plans to build new schools. Similar problems happened in Virginia, where classrooms for black students were so overcrowded that some had to hold classes on school buses. These cases became an important part of the civil rights movement that was gaining ground during the 1950s.

Brown v. Board of Education was actually made up of five civil rights cases. Gardner Bishop, involved in a case called *Bolling v. Melvin Sharpe*, is shown projected on a screen at a conference.

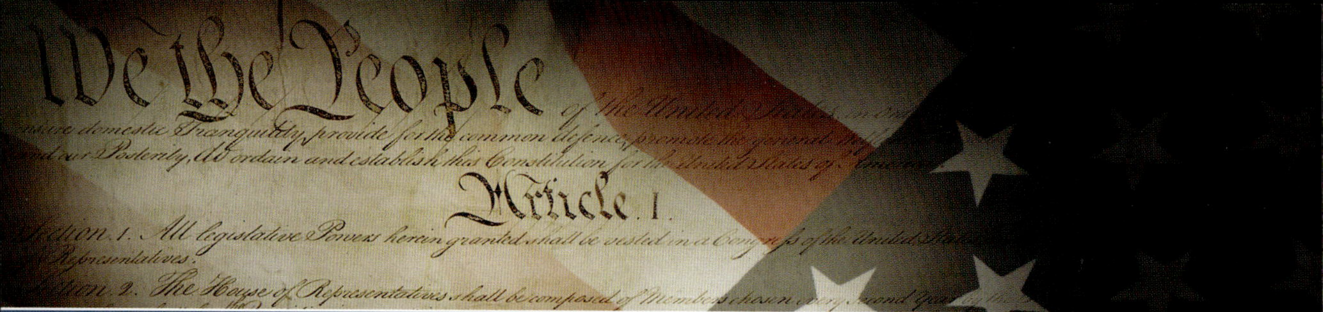

THE HISTORY OF EDUCATION FOR AFRICAN AMERICANS

Many people, especially in the southern states, did not want blacks and whites to attend the same schools. After the Civil War, in the late 1800s and early 1900s, slavery had been outlawed, but still many southern states discouraged the education of black children. Even when black children did get an education, they got it at schools separate from whites. Schools for black children received little funding. By discouraging these children from receiving an education, some residents and even state governments hoped they would work in fields or serve as domestic servants when they were adults. They worried about who would do these jobs if African Americans didn't want to.

African American children pose in front of their South Carolina schoolhouse with their white teachers in 1862. The students are freed slaves.

While badly maintained schools became a symbol of the poor treatment of blacks, there were also some advances in black education. The Civil War era was a time when high-quality colleges for African Americans were founded. Many of these prestigious schools still exist today.

THE EQUAL PROTECTION CLAUSE

The Supreme Court judges who were considering the *Brown v. Board of Education* case in 1956 had an important job to do. They had to determine if African American children were being denied rights that white children were being given.

The Fourteenth Amendment to the Constitution directs the government to protect people's rights under the law. It says in part, "No state shall… deprive any person of life, liberty, or property, without due process of law; nor deny to any person within its jurisdiction the equal protection of the laws."

This part of the amendment has become known as the "equal protection" clause. The amendment was passed in 1868, soon after the Civil War. It was meant to protect the rights of the people who

Some of the attorneys involved in *Brown v. Board of Education* are shown here. From left to right, they are Thurgood Marshall, Louis Redding, and U. Simpson Tate.

had been freed from slavery. But though it was set in law, it was not tested until Supreme Court cases that came later. In the meantime, African Americans suffered from discrimination and segregation.

WHY WAS THE CASE IMPORTANT?

The case of *Brown v. Board of Education* was one of the most important Supreme Court decisions of the civil rights movement. At the time the case was being considered in the 1950s, the country was divided on the topic. Many whites did not understand the problems blacks faced, while others wanted to keep laws and practices the way they were. But civil rights activists held protests to demand more rights for African Americans. They protested the "separate but equal" laws, "whites only" swimming pools and water fountains, and other forms of segregation and discrimination. Dr. Martin Luther King Jr. and Rosa Parks were at the forefront of efforts to stop the segregation of city buses in Montgomery, Alabama. Civil rights leaders led peaceful marches to protest the injustice they were suffering. Protesters' actions

More than fifteen thousand people marched on Washington, DC, in 1959 in support of school integration.

were getting noticed across the nation. The civil rights movement grew in both the North and the South.

Civil rights activists felt that one of the most important things they could do to improve future race relations was to improve conditions for the young. If schools remained segregated, black children would grow up feeling inferior to white children. They would not feel welcome in the society they would inherit when they grew up. Activists argued that the Constitution was written for all Americans, not just white ones. If black families could not assure their children that the Constitution and the amendments applied to them, then America would not be doing its job to protect the rights of all people.

Some people felt that the best way to break the cycle of racism in America would be to make the next generation of African Americans equal to whites. That meant not being kept in separate schools, mixing all races, each as citizens with the same rights under the law.

Linda Brown is shown in the doorway of this school bus. Her legal case against public schools in 1953 was a landmark civil rights case in the United States.

THE DECISION

After three years of discussing the *Brown v. Board of Education* case, the Supreme Court finally made its decision. On May 17, 1954, the court handed down a unanimous decision that stated that segregated schools and separate facilities for different races was unconstitutional. The court explained that the overcrowding and lack of funding to all-black schools created an inferior educational experience that would affect the outcome of the children's lives. Segregation interfered with their ability to function in American society. On May 31, 1955, the court issued more direction on their decision. Schools were ordered to end segregation "with all deliberate speed."

Thurgood Marshall made a major contribution to the court's decision. As the top lawyer for the National Association for the Advancement of Colored People (NAACP), he fought for the civil rights of African Americans. He argued the case in front of the Supreme Court successfully. More than a decade later, Marshall was named as the first African American judge in the Supreme Court.

Attorney Thurgood Marshall worked on the *Brown v. Board of Education* case as well as many others that involved the civil rights of African American citizens.

CHIEF JUSTICE EARL WARREN

Each time the Supreme Court makes a decision, one of the judges presents the decision to the court and explains why he or she thinks the decision is fair. In the case of *Brown v. Board of Education*, Chief Justice Earl Warren wrote his ideas about the case. He explained that the "separate but equal" idea from the Fourteenth Amendment was referring to transportation, not education. He did not think the founders of the nation meant to keep children separated and unequal as they were getting their education.

In part of his argument, he wrote: "Segregation of white and colored children in public schools has a detrimental effect upon the colored children. The impact is greater when it has the sanction of the law … We conclude that in the field of public education the doctrine of 'separate but equal' has no place. Separate educational facilities are inherently unequal."

Another important person in the *Brown v. Board of Education* case was Chief Justice Earl Warren. He presented the case and explained the court's decision.

THE RESULTS

The Supreme Court judges ruled unanimously that schools should not be segregated. However, the reaction around the nation was far from unanimous. Many people cheered the decision. They felt that it was long overdue and that the efforts to fight for equality were paying off. Others were angry that such a large change would be coming to their schools. The decision affected many people, especially throughout the South. White people there were especially emotional about the decision. Some of them did not think that blacks and whites were equal, and they did not want black children attending school with their white children. The *Brown v. Board of Education* decision would have a big effect on many people's lives.

News of the Supreme Court's decision spread across the nation quickly. It would go on to have a great impact on African American children all over the country.

The fact that *Plessy v. Ferguson* was overturned, or reversed, showed the direction the civil rights movement was headed. Not everyone agreed with the decision, and the debates became even more heated.

Not everyone agreed with the court's decision. Arkansas governor Orval Faubus blocked African American students from entering a high school in Little Rock.

In the years that followed, the results of the case had lasting effects. The process of desegregation, or students of all races attending schools, took years to complete. Protesters objected loudly—and sometimes violently.

In 1957, nine black students enrolled in Little Rock Central High School, an all-white school in Little Rock, Arkansas. The governor of Arkansas, Orval Faubus, kept the students from entering the school by using the state's National Guard. In addition, angry protesters outside the school met the students with racist shouting.

The incident gained national attention, but the problem continued until President Dwight D. Eisenhower ordered the US Army to make sure the students could enter the school. The case of the Little Rock Nine is one example of the difficulties that African Americans faced now that the ending of segregation allowed them to claim their rightful places in schools across the nation.

EFFECTS ON THE CIVIL RIGHTS MOVEMENT

The rest of the 1950s brought many growing pains and lessons in respect and tolerance to the United States. In 1955, Montgomery, Alabama, resident Rosa Parks was arrested for sitting in the "whites-only" section of a city bus. Her arrest brought attention to the issue of segregation. Dr. Martin Luther King Jr. led a boycott of the Montgomery bus system that lasted thirteen months, until the laws were finally changed. Boycotts continued around the country. By 1960, protests had grown to be nationwide. On February 1, 1960, four black students from a college in North Carolina sat at a lunch counter meant only for whites to protest discrimination.

Stores like this Woolworth became a place where peaceful protests called sit-ins took place. The events protested the separation of blacks and whites in public places.

Protests and boycotts led to people being arrested. In addition to court rulings like *Brown v. Board of Education*, these forms of civil disobedience played a big part in changing "separate but equal" laws around the country.

HOW SCHOOLS HAVE CHANGED

Since the *Brown v. Board of Education* decision, American schools have changed a great deal. Today, people of all races attend school together, and they are all protected equally under the law.

In the southern states, racism was widespread in the 1950s. Segregated schools meant that children of different races had few opportunities to be friends with each other. Desegregation meant that black students and white students would be in the same classes together and play together on the playground. Before desegregation, it was difficult for students of different races to realize that they are all equal to each other. The combination of children of different races attending school together benefited all the children socially.

Schools all across the United States had to deal with the challenges of discrimination while desegregating schools and integrating students of different races.

Making a higher quality of education available to children of all races meant that black children would grow up to have opportunities similar to those of white children.

Areas with high populations of minorities still face issues of poverty and crime, like this neighborhood in Miami Beach, Florida.

Although *Brown v. Board of Education* helped make educational opportunities equal under the law, it did not fix all the problems of African American students. Even decades later, many black families are still faced with issues of poverty. Black students often go to schools that do not perform as well as schools in richer neighborhoods. Schools with large black populations often face lack of funding, overcrowding, and violence, all of which distracts from student learning on a daily basis.

According to the US Census Bureau, 39 percent of black children are from families with incomes below the poverty line. This is true of only 12 percent of white children. The issue of unequal social status is one of the civil rights struggles that people are facing today. The problem of poverty is more difficult to fix than the issue of desegregation of schools.

HOW ELSE DOES THE SUPREME COURT HELP WITH CIVIL RIGHTS?

The Supreme Court plays a very important role in shaping the lives of American citizens. Often, people do not even realize the role that the courts have played in their everyday lives. Students today are decades away from the world their grandparents lived in during the civil rights movement. They have opportunities their grandparents did not have.

While the courts have helped make life better and fairer, they continue to review civil rights cases every year. Today's civil rights issues may not be just about the rights of African Americans. The courts have considered cases about same sex marriage and the rights of transgender individuals. Courts continue to analyze cases of discrimination involving race and gender. In each case, the

Civil rights cases that the Supreme Court deals with today are concerned with more than just race. Some involve same-sex marriage or discrimination regarding sexual orientation.

judges consider what was meant by the wording in the Constitution. They look at previous cases that were similar. The discussion between them helps them reach a fair and unbiased opinion.

LOOKING AHEAD TO NEW CIVIL RIGHTS LAWS

The civil rights struggles of Americans are far from over. The progress made during the 1950s and 1960s was enormous. But the struggles continue, and there is a lot more progress needed. The organization of the US government, however, makes it possible to change laws as times change and different issues of fairness arise in society. Arguments that cannot be settled by state courts will continue to go to the Supreme Court. Unfair legislation will continue to be changed.

Some new civil rights cases involve the rights of citizens when they are stopped by the police. New cases are sent to the Supreme Court on a regular basis. With each new decision made

Monroe Elementary School in Topeka, Kansas, is the location of the *Brown v. Board of Education* National Historic Site. It is a reminder of the landmark civil rights case and its impact on the nation.

by the nation's courts, some citizens react with strong emotion. Just as happened with *Brown v. Board of Education*, the nation will change and grow with every new decision.

GLOSSARY

amendment A change to a document.

Bill of Rights The first ten amendments to the US Constitution, which guaranteed rights such as the freedom of speech and religion.

boycott To refuse to buy or take part in something to show a disagreement or to protest.

civil rights The rights of citizens to equal rights.

Constitution The document ratified in 1788 establishing the basic laws and rights of US citizens.

desegregation The end of a period of separation, particularly regarding racial segregation.

detrimental Harmful.

discrimination The unjust treatment of a particular group, especially if it is based on race, age, or gender.

doctrine A set of beliefs.

executive branch The branch of the US government responsible for supporting and enforcing laws.

judicial branch The branch of the US government responsible for interpreting laws.

legislative branch The branch of the US government responsible for creating laws.

overturned Reversed or changed to have an opposite effect.

racism Unfair treatment or prejudice toward a particular racial group.

sanction An official permission or approval.

segregation The action of separating or setting apart.

Supreme Court The highest judicial court in the United States.

unanimous Fully agreed upon by all parties or given the same vote by all parties.

Alliance for Justice (AFJ)
11 Dupont Circle NW, 2nd Floor
Washington, DC 20036
(202) 822-6070
Website: http://www.afj.org
Facebook: @AllianceforJustice
Twitter: @AFJustice
Instagram: @alliancecompassion
AFJ represents civil rights and social justice organizations.

American Civil Liberties Union (ACLU)
125 Broad Street, 18th Floor
New York, NY 10004
(212) 549-2500
Website: https://www.aclu.org
Facebook: @aclu.nationwide
Twitter: @ACLU
Instagram: @aclu_nationwide
The ACLU is an organization that defends through advocacy work the individual rights and liberties guaranteed by the US Constitution.

Canada Civil Liberties Association (CCLA)
90 Eglinton Ave. E, Suite 900
Toronto, ON M4P 1A6
Canada
(416) 363-0321
Website: https://ccla.org
Facebook: @BCCivLib
Twitter: @cancivlib

Instagram: @civlib
The CCLA fights for civil liberties and human rights and freedoms for all Canadians.

National Association for the Advancement of Colored People (NAACP)
4805 Mt. Hope Drive
Baltimore, MD 21215
(877) 622-2798
Website: http://www.naacp.org
Facebook: @naacp
Twitter: @NAACP
Instagram: @naacp
The NAACP works to defend citizens' right and prevents racial discrimination.

United States Department of Justice (DOJ)
900 Pennsylvania Avenue, NW
Washington, DC 20530
(800) 877-8339
Website: https://www.justice.gov
Facebook: @DOJ
Twitter: @TheJusticeDept
Instagram: @thejusticedept
The DOJ is the part of the US government that enforces laws.

WEBSITES

Because of the changing nature of internet links, Rosen Publishing has developed an online list of websites related to the subject of this book. This site is updated regularly. Please use this link to access this list:

http://www.rosenlinks.com/SCRM/Brown

FOR FURTHER READING

Compston, Christine L. Earl Warren: *Justice for All*. Oxford, UK: Oxford University Press, 2002.

Deibel, Zachary. *Thurgood Marshall and Brown v. Board of Education of Topeka*. New York, NY: Cavendish Square Publishing, 2016.

Jeffrey, Gary. *Thurgood Marshall: The Supreme Court Rules on "Separate but Equal."* New York, NY: Gareth Stevens Publishing, 2012.

Levinson, Cynthia. *The Youngest Marcher: The Story of Audrey Faye Hendricks, a Young Civil Rights Activist*. New York, NY: Atheneum Books for Young Readers, 2017.

Lit, Ira W. *The Bus Kids: Children's Experiences with Voluntary Desegregation*. New Haven, CT: Yale University Press, 2009.

Rappaport, Doreen, and Curtis James. *The School Is Not White: A True Story of the Civil Rights Movement*. Concord, MA: StarWalk Kids Media, 2014.

Rubin, Susan Goldman. *Brown v. Board of Education: A Fight for Simple Justice*. New York, NY: Holiday House, 2016.

Whitelaw, Nancy. *Supreme Court Justices: Thurgood Marshall*. Greensboro, NC: Morgan Reynolds Publishing, 2010.

BIBLIOGRAPHY

Foner, Eric, and John A. Garraty. *The Reader's Companion to American History*. New York, NY: Houghton Mifflin Harcourt Publishing Company, 1991.

Johnson, Berman E. "Supreme Court Decisions that Changed America." American Association of Community Colleges. Retrieved March 2, 2017. http://www.aacc.nche.edu/Resources/aaccprograms/diversity/brownvboard/Pages/supremecourt.aspx.

Leadership Conference, The. "Brown v. Board of Education (Kansas)." Retrieved March 2, 2017. http://www.civilrights.org/education/brown/brown.html.

Leadership Conference, The. "Important Supreme Court Cases for Civil Rights." Retrieved March 2, 2017. http://www.civilrights.org/judiciary/supreme-court/key-cases.html.

National Park Service. "Brown v. Board of Education: History & Culture" Retrieved March 2, 2017. https://www.nps.gov/brvb/learn/historyculture/index.htm.

Smolin, David. "Equal Protection." The Heritage Guide to the Constitution. Retrieved March 2, 2017. http://www.heritage.org/constitution/#!/amendments/14/essays/171/equal-protection.

Virginia Historical Society. "Beginnings of Black Education." Retrieved March 2, 2017. http://www.vahistorical.org/collections-and-resources/virginia-history-explorer/civil-rights-movement-virginia/beginnings-black.

ABOUT THE AUTHOR

Kathy Furgang has written dozens of books for young readers, including books about amendments to the US Constitution and the life of Rosa Parks. She graduated from Fordham University and lives in upstate New York with her husband and two sons.

PHOTO CREDITS

Cover, pp. 1, 11, 23 Carl Iwasaki/The LIFE Images Collection /Getty Images; pp. 3, 42, 43, 45, 46, 47 Onur Ersin/Shutterstock .com; pp. 4, 6, 8, 10, 12, 14, 16, 18, 20, 24, 26, 28, 32, 34, 38, 40, back cover Sergey Kamshylin/Shutterstock.com; p. 5 larry1235 /Shutterstock.com; pp. 7–13 Everett Historical/Shutterstock.com; pp. 9, 15 © AP Images; pp. 17, 25 Library of Congress Prints and Photographs Division; p. 19 AP Photo/Courtesy of the NAACP; pp. 21, 29, 31, 35 Bettmann/Getty Images; pp. 27, 33 © iStockphoto. com/traveler1116; p. 37 © iStockphoto.com/TasfotoNL; p. 39 Rena Schild/Shutterstock.com; p. 41 tomorrowspix/iStock/Thinkstock.

Design: Nelson Sá; Editor and Photo Researcher: Xina M. Uhl